Fun Letter Tracing Book
━For Preschoolers━

©Angela McBride. All rights reserved. No part of this publication may be reproduced, redistributed or transmitted, in any form, including photocopying, recording, or other electronic or mechanical methods without the prior written permission of the publisher, except in the case of brief quotations embodied in reviews and certain other non-commercial uses permitted by copyright law.
Credits: The cover and some interior images designed by www.Freepik.com

Without your thoughts, there is no me.
Kindly support me and leave a review on Amazon.
Thank You!

PART I
LETTER TRACING

Trace and color the alphabets

A is for Apple

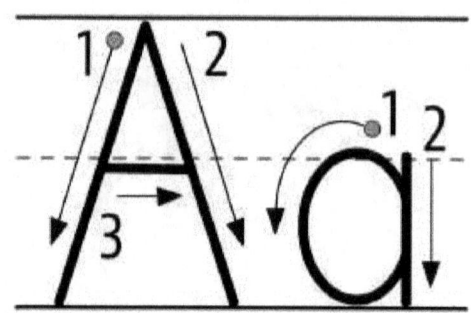

I Know My Letter:

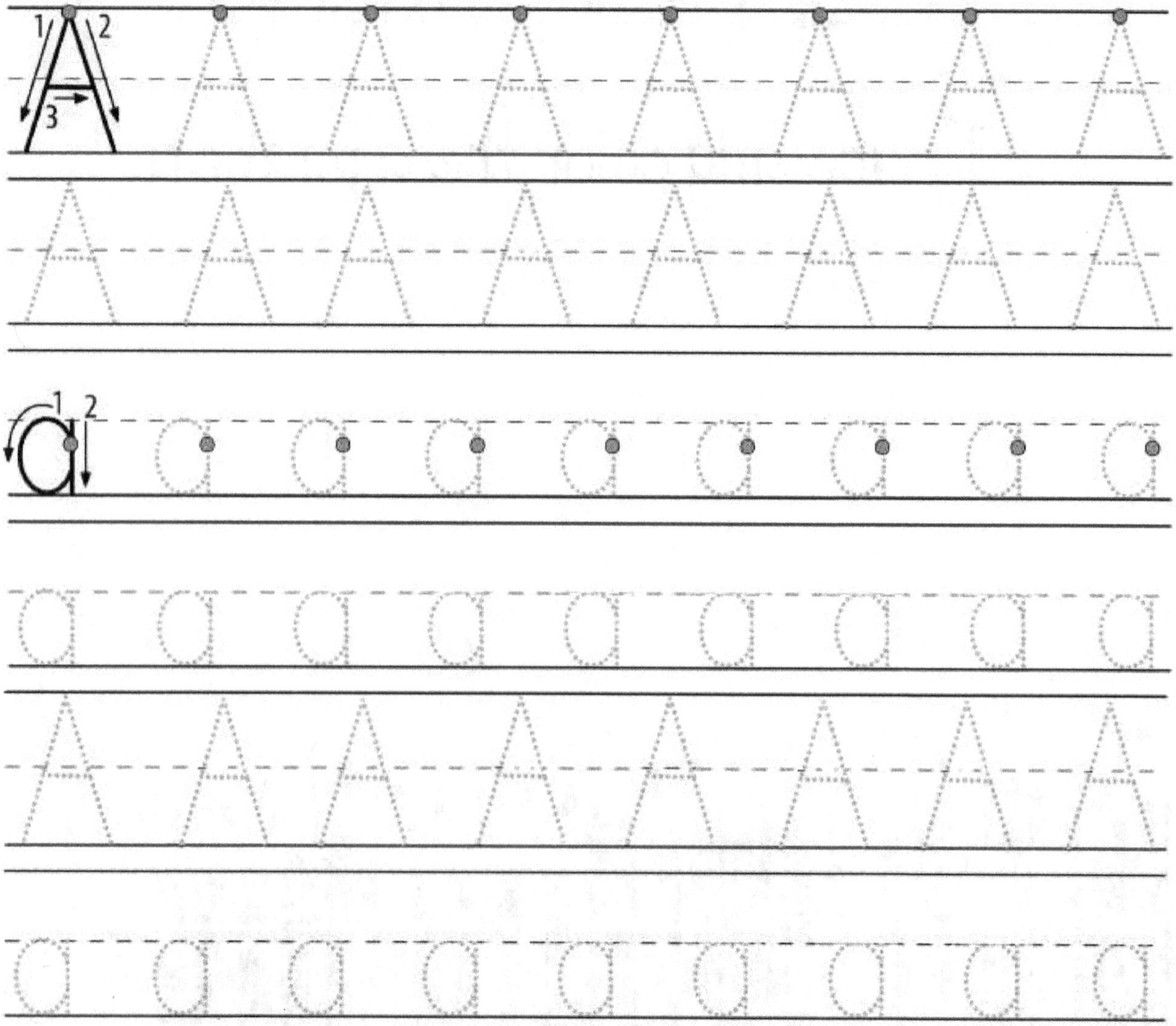

PRACTICE!   PRACTICE!   PRACTICE!

Ambulance

Airplane

Trace and Color

PRACTICE! PRACTICE! PRACTICE!

B is for Bus

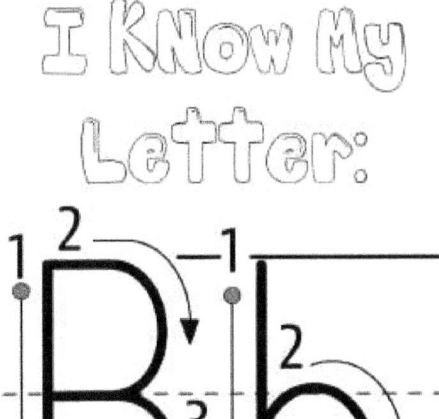

I Know My Letter:

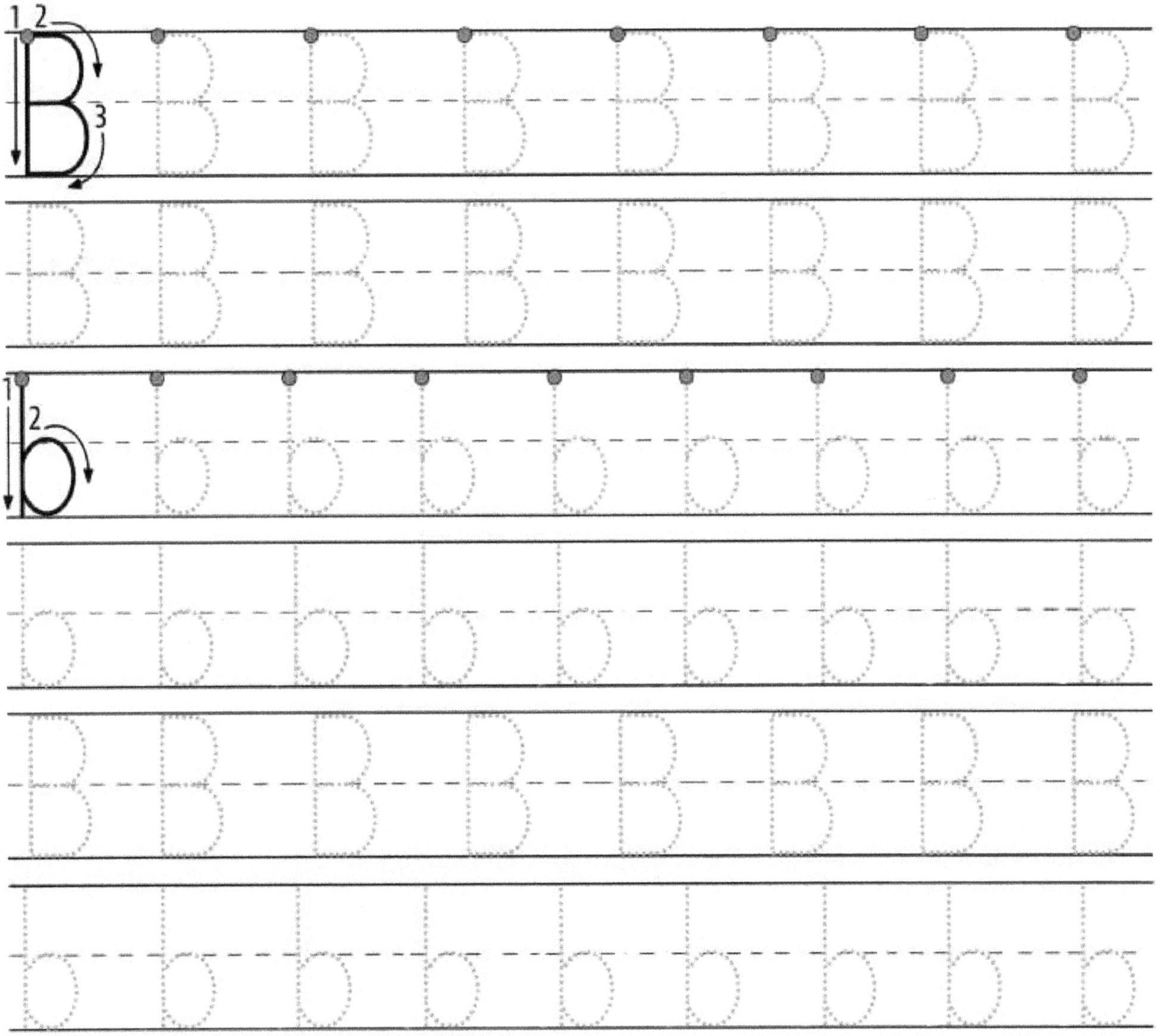

PRACTICE!   PRACTICE!   PRACTICE!

Bee

Banana

Trace and Color

B

PRACTICE! PRACTICE! PRACTICE!

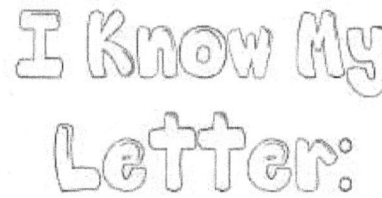

I Know My Letter:

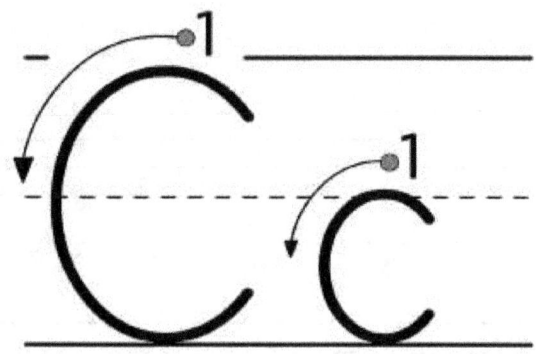

C is for Car

PRACTICE!   PRACTICE!   PRACTICE!

Chicken

Cake

Trace and Color

C

PRACTICE! PRACTICE! PRACTICE!

D is for Drum

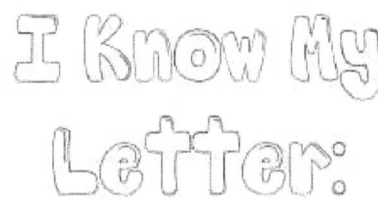

I Know My Letter:

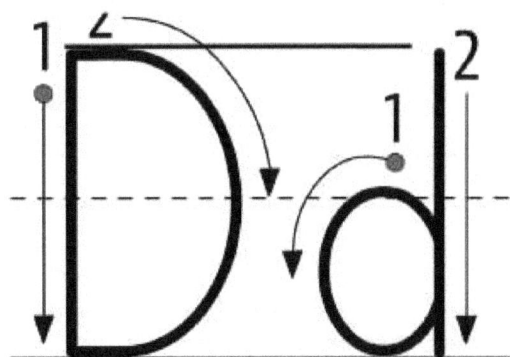

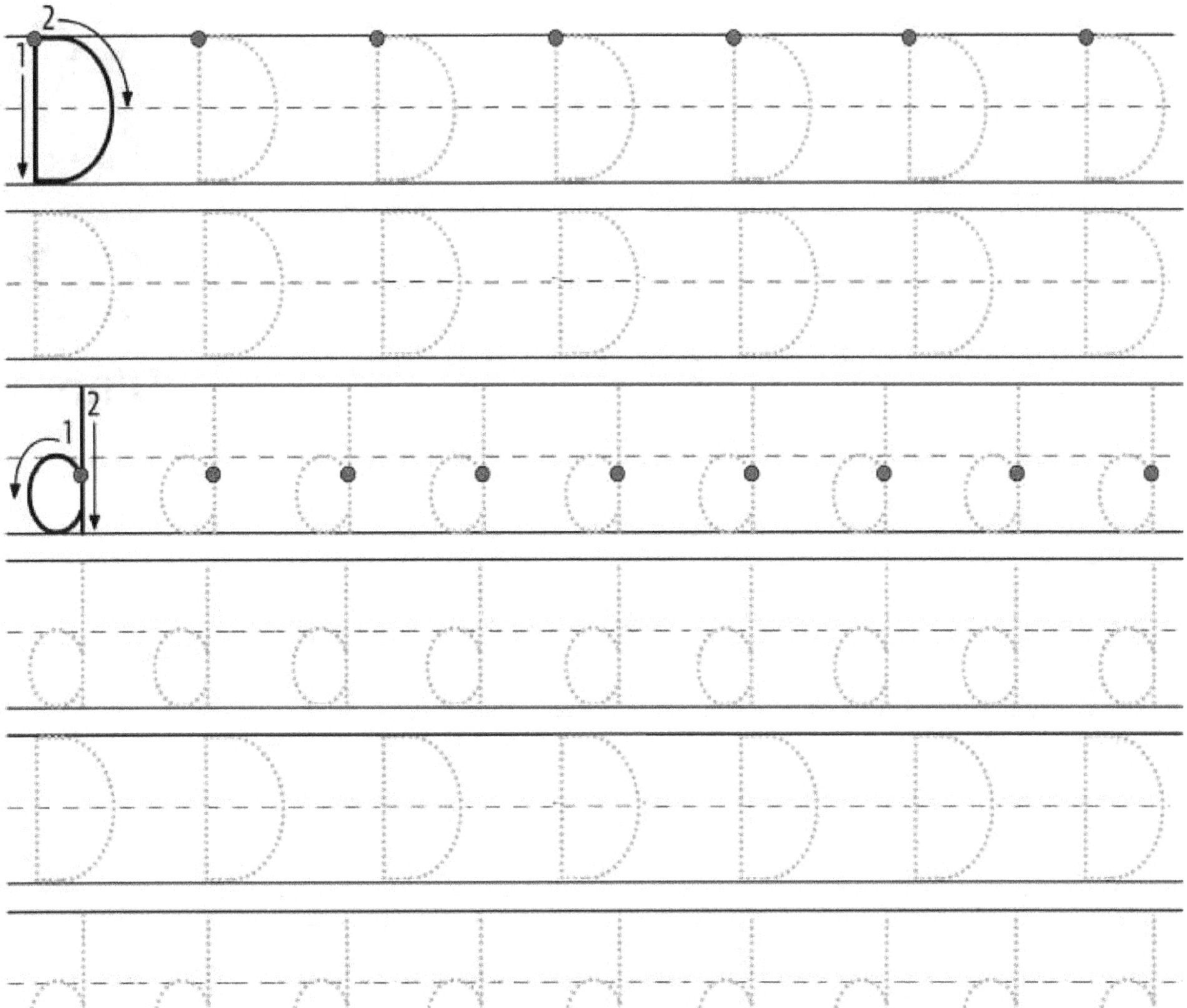

PRACTICE! PRACTICE! PRACTICE!

Door

Dinosaur

Trace and Color

PRACTICE! PRACTICE! PRACTICE!

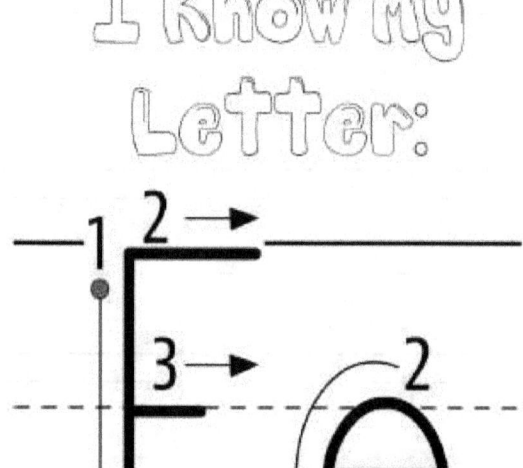

I Know My Letter:

E is for Elephant

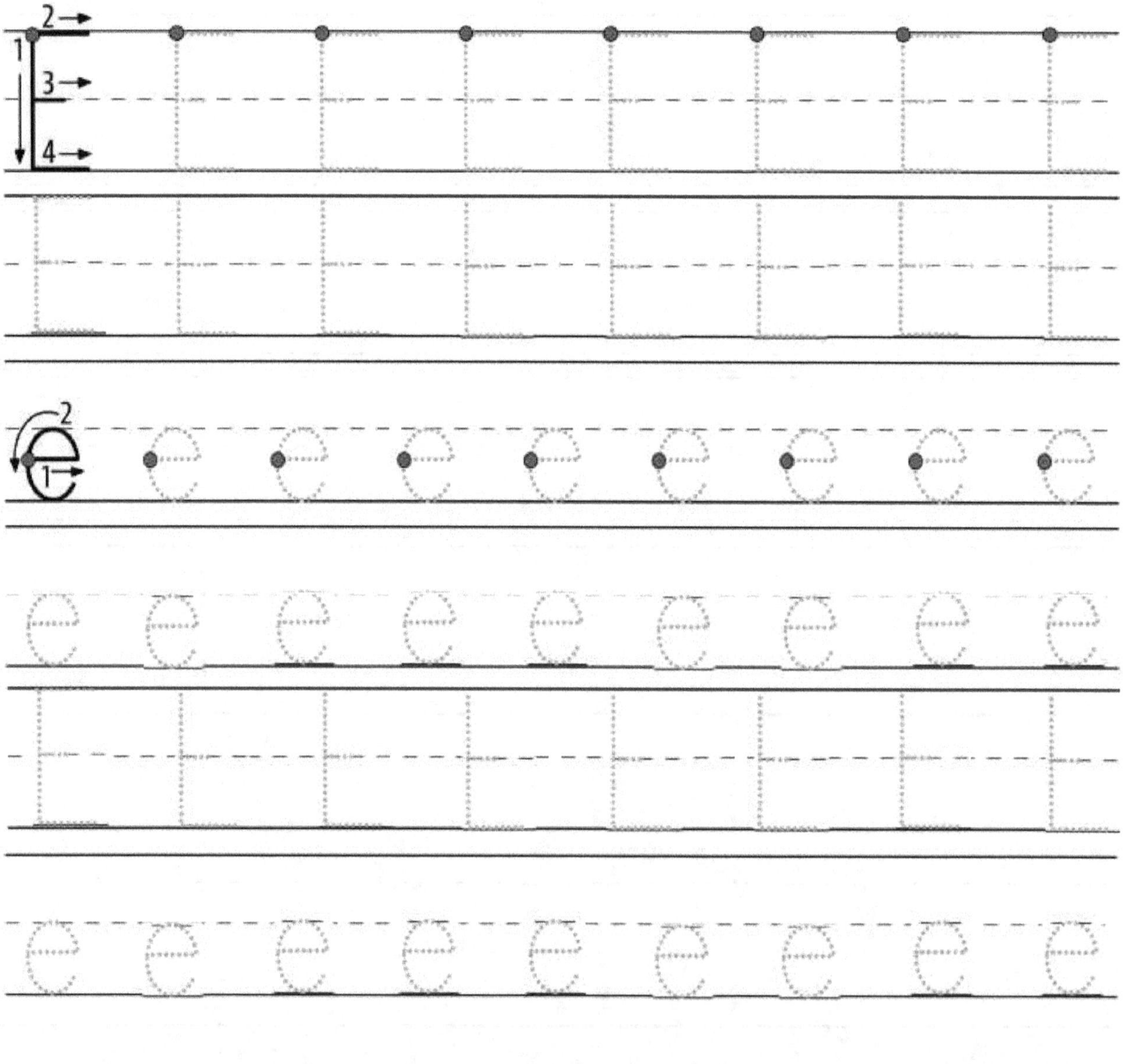

PRACTICE! PRACTICE! PRACTICE!

Egg

Elf

Trace and Color

PRACTICE! PRACTICE! PRACTICE!

F is for Flower

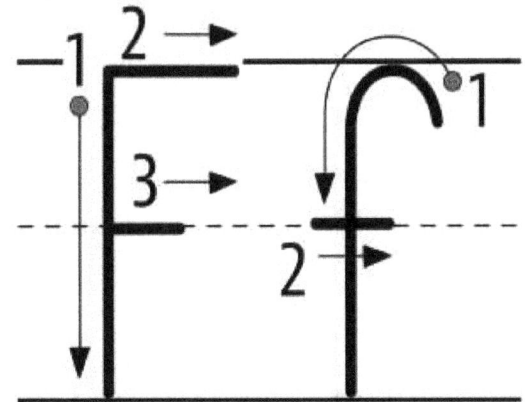

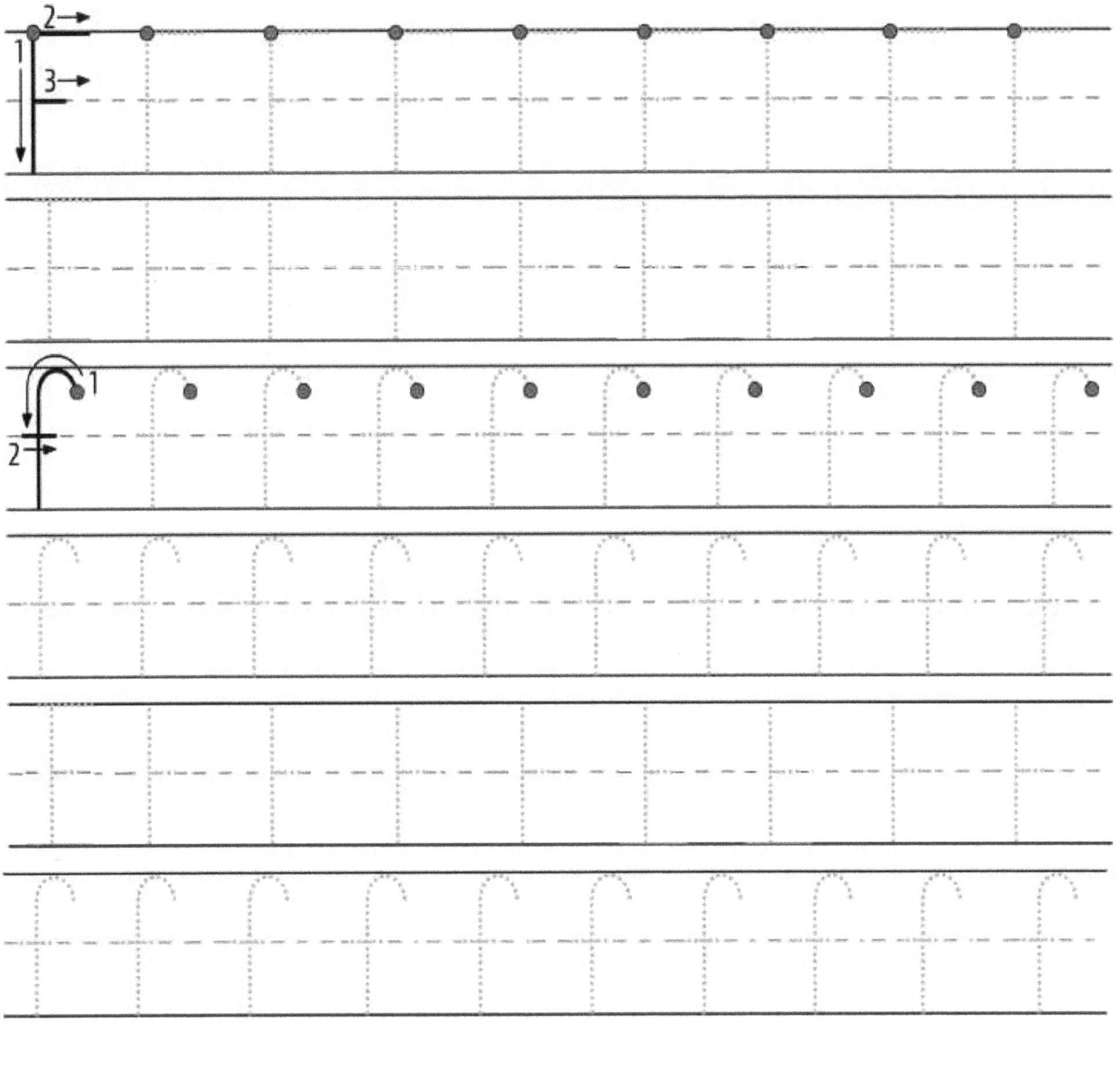

PRACTICE! PRACTICE! PRACTICE!

Fence

Fox

Trace and Color

F

PRACTICE! PRACTICE! PRACTICE!

G is for Goat

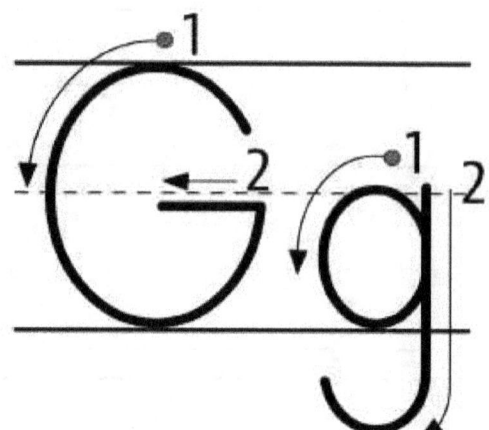

I Know My Letter:

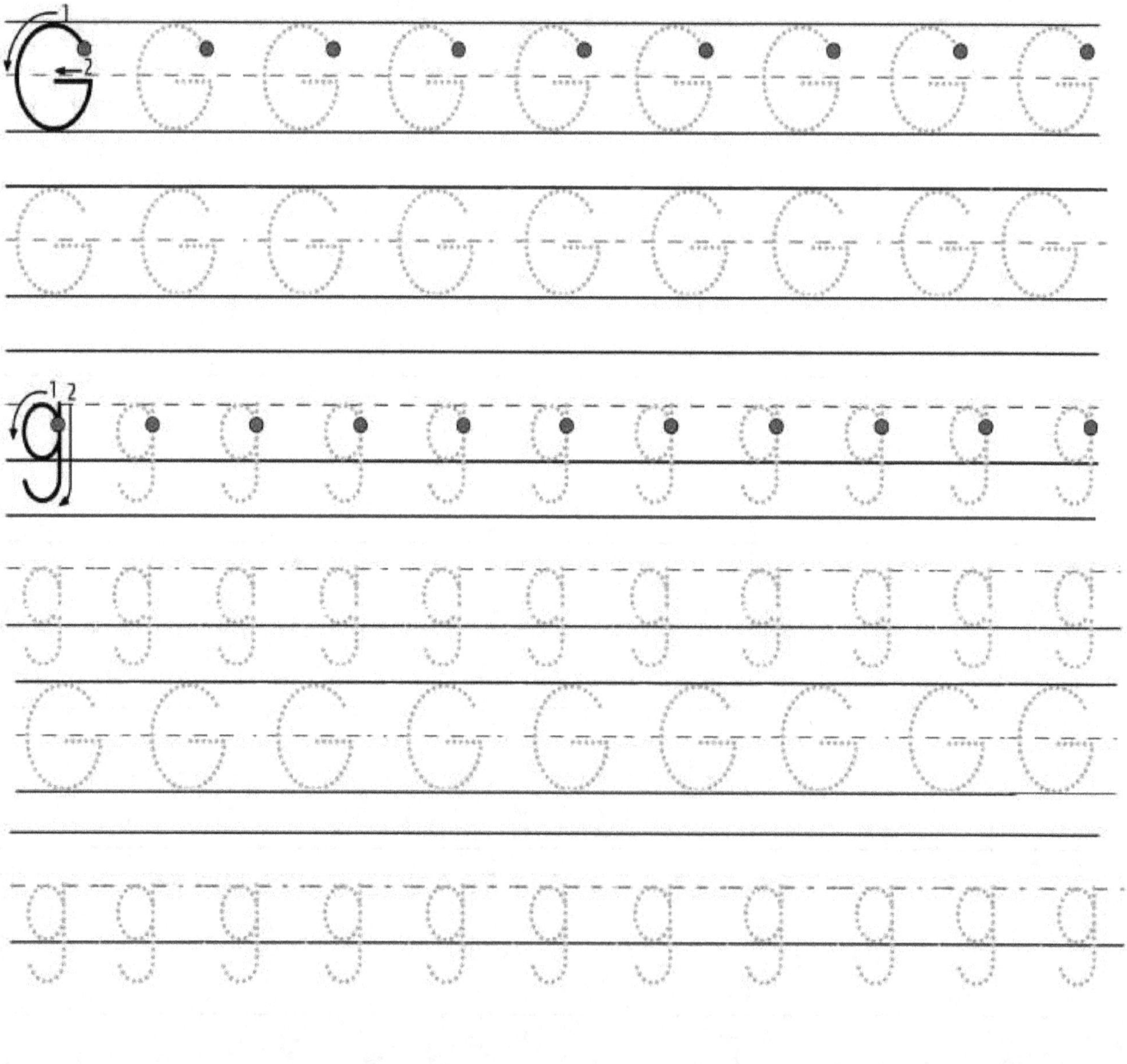

PRACTICE!   PRACTICE!   PRACTICE!

Garbage Can

Giraffe

Trace and Color

PRACTICE! PRACTICE! PRACTICE!

H is for House

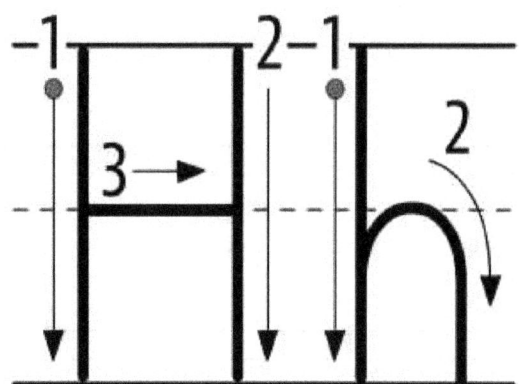

I Know My Letter:

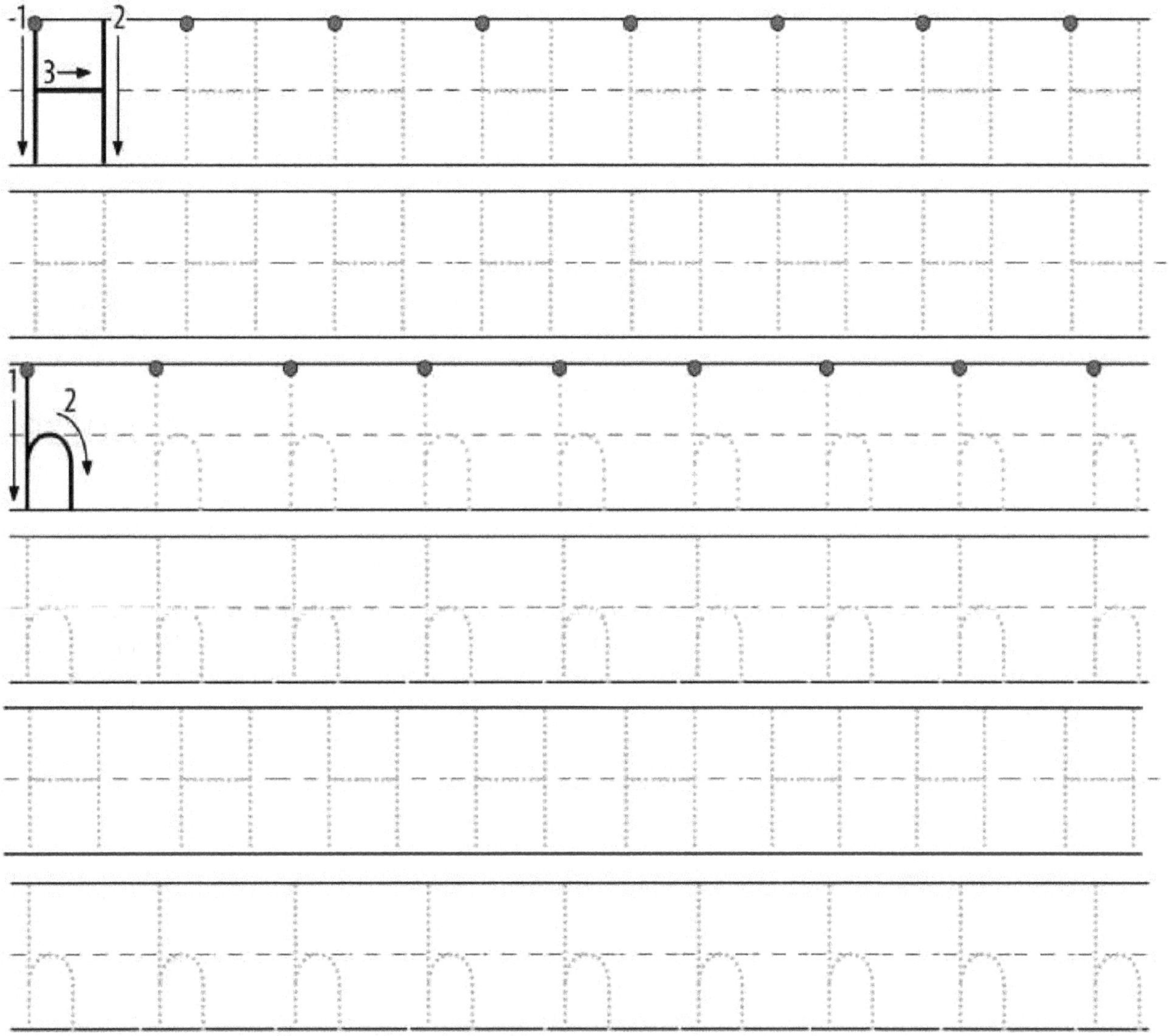

PRACTICE! PRACTICE! PRACTICE!

Hat

Horse

Trace and Color

PRACTICE! PRACTICE! PRACTICE!

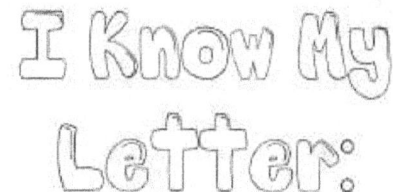

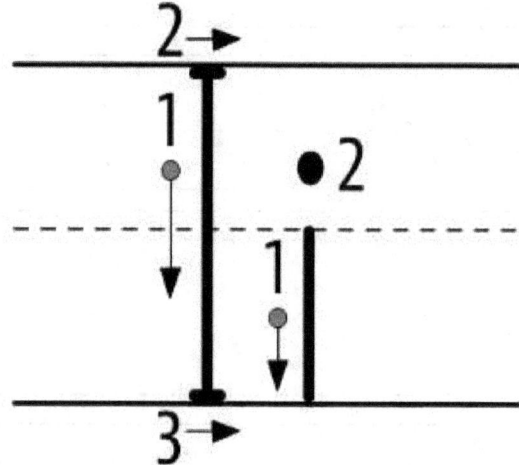

I is for Ice cream

PRACTICE! PRACTICE! PRACTICE!

Iguana

Igloo

Trace and Color

PRACTICE! PRACTICE! PRACTICE!

J is for Jellyfish

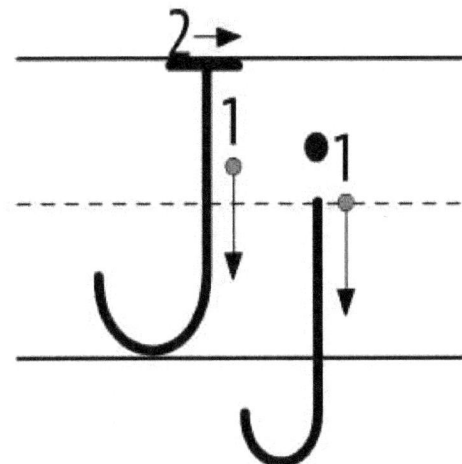

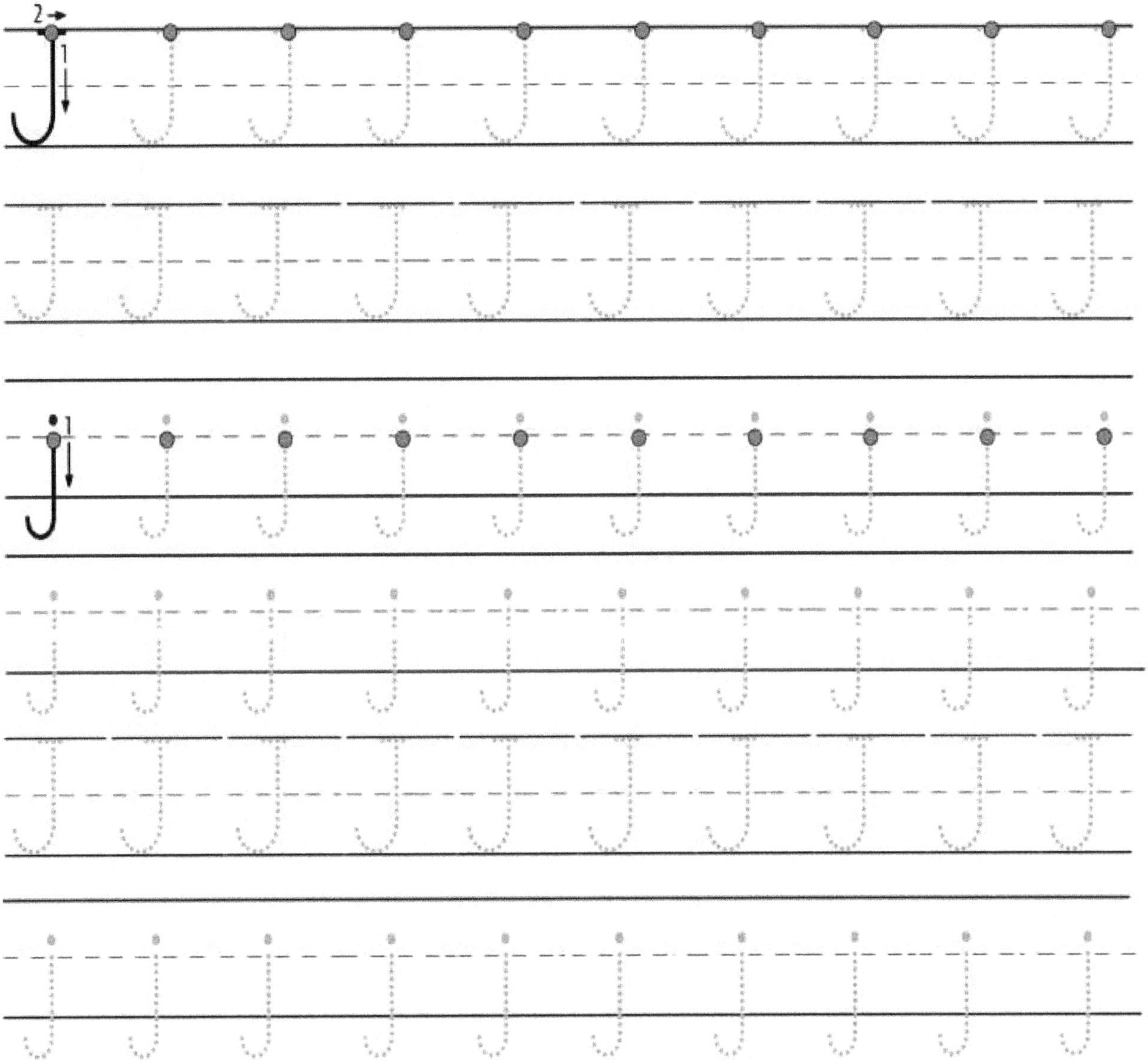

PRACTICE! PRACTICE! PRACTICE!

Jug

Jigsaw

Trace and Color

PRACTICE! PRACTICE! PRACTICE!

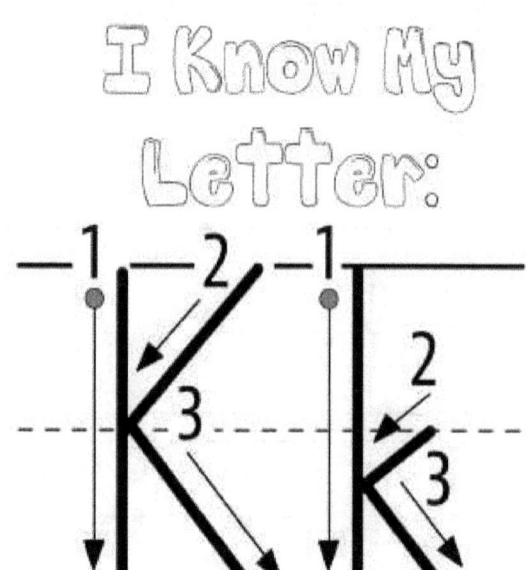

K is for Kite

PRACTICE! PRACTICE! PRACTICE!

Kettle

Kangaroo

Trace and Color

PRACTICE! PRACTICE! PRACTICE!

L is for Lion

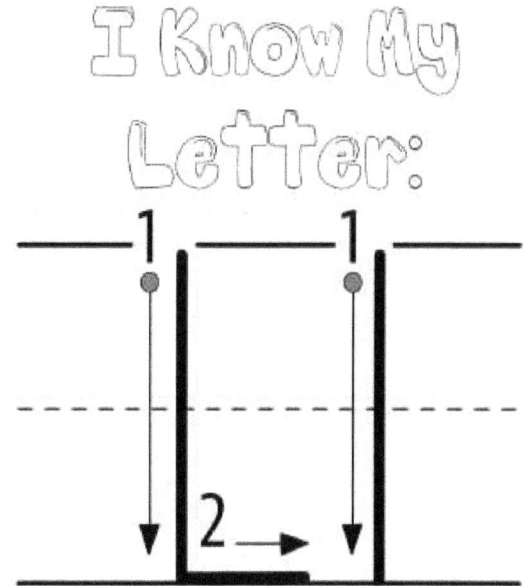

PRACTICE! PRACTICE! PRACTICE!

Log

Lemon

Trace and Color

PRACTICE! PRACTICE! PRACTICE!

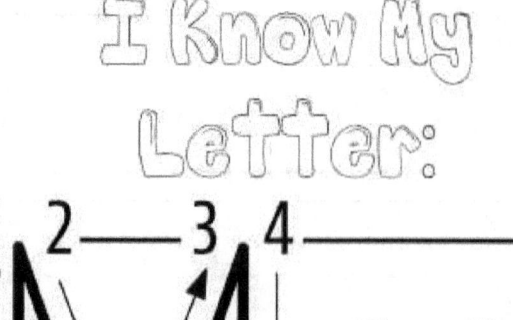

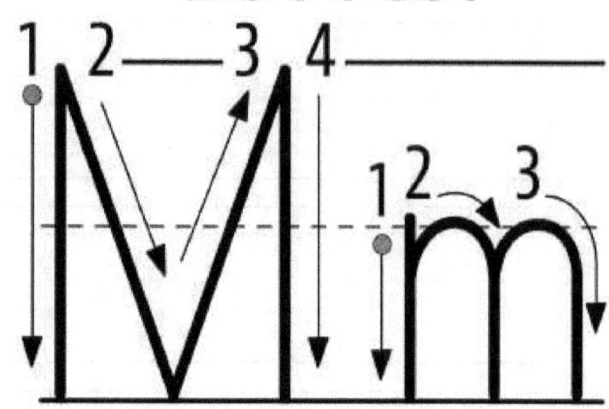

M is for Monkey

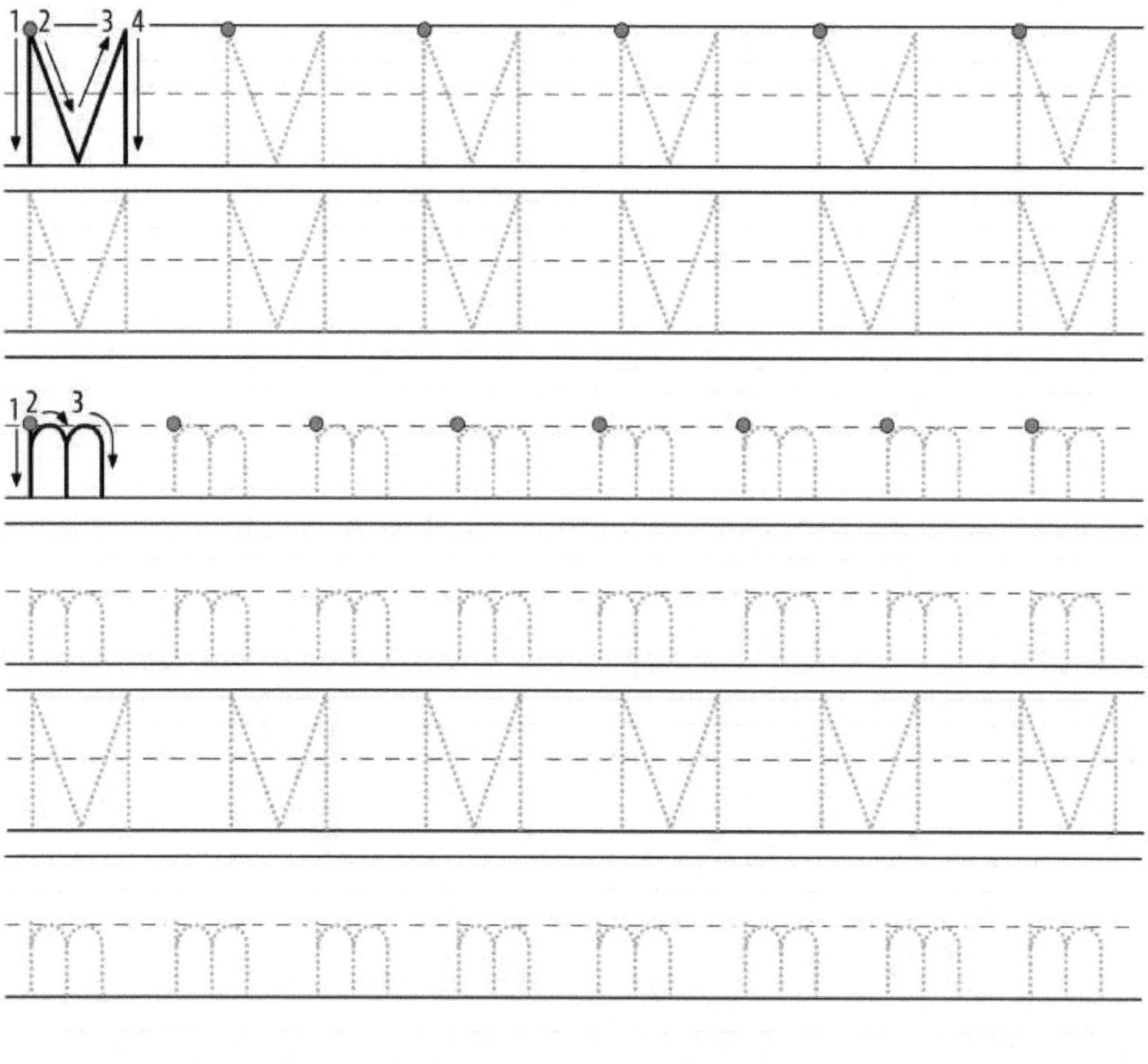

PRACTICE! PRACTICE! PRACTICE!

Mask

Mango

Trace and Color

M

PRACTICE! PRACTICE! PRACTICE!

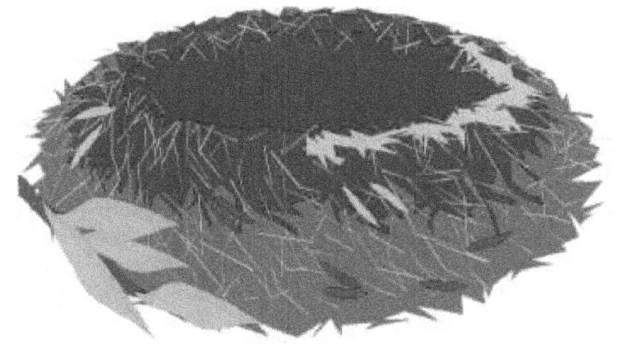
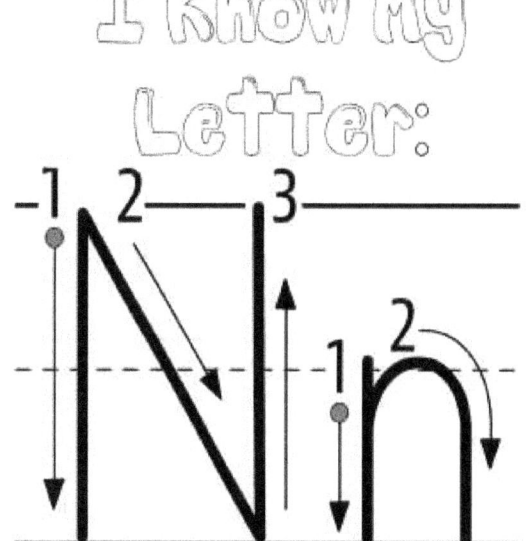

N is for Nest

PRACTICE! PRACTICE! PRACTICE!

Necklace

Newt

Trace and Color

N

PRACTICE!   PRACTICE!   PRACTICE!

O is for Owl

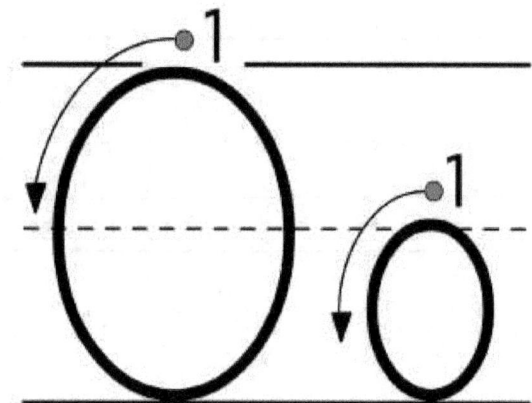

I Know My Letter:

PRACTICE! PRACTICE! PRACTICE!

Orange

Ox

Trace and Color

PRACTICE! PRACTICE! PRACTICE!

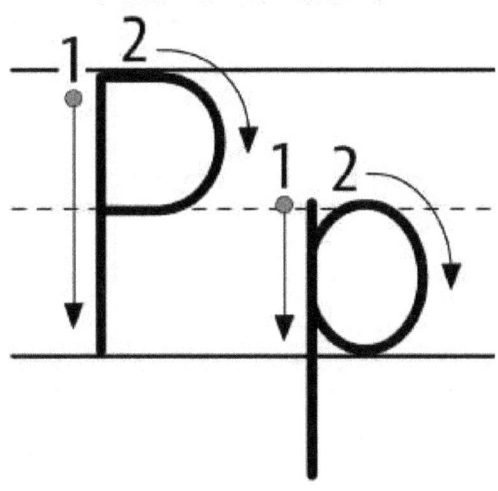

P is for Pencil

PRACTICE!   PRACTICE!   PRACTICE!

Pig

Pineapple

Trace and Color

PRACTICE!   PRACTICE!   PRACTICE!

I Know My Letter:

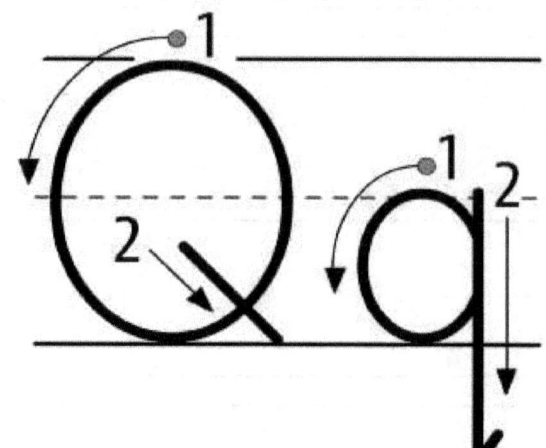

Q is for Queen

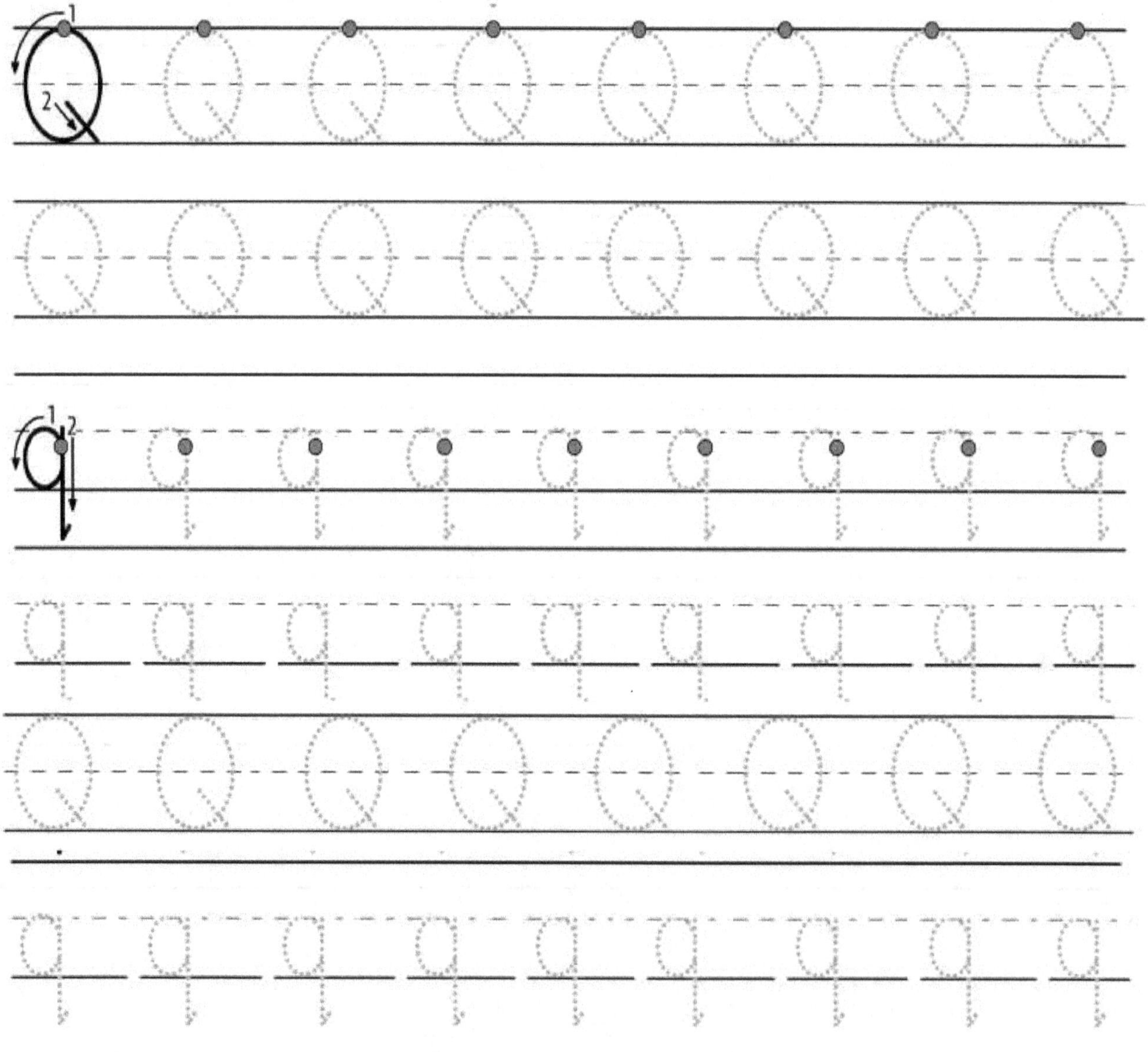

PRACTICE! PRACTICE! PRACTICE!

Quilt

Quail

Trace and Color

PRACTICE! PRACTICE! PRACTICE!

R is for Raspberry

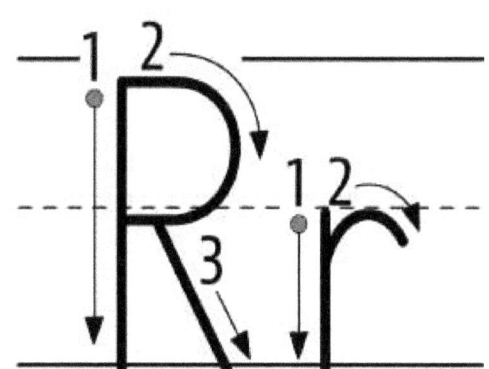

I Know My Letter:

PRACTICE!   PRACTICE!   PRACTICE!

Rabbit

Rainbow

Trace and Color

PRACTICE! PRACTICE! PRACTICE!

S is for Snake

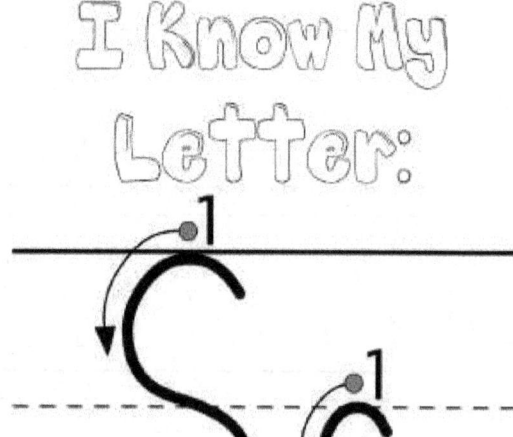

I Know My Letter:

PRACTICE!   PRACTICE!   PRACTICE!

Star

Strawberry

Trace and Color

S

PRACTICE! PRACTICE! PRACTICE!

T is for Table

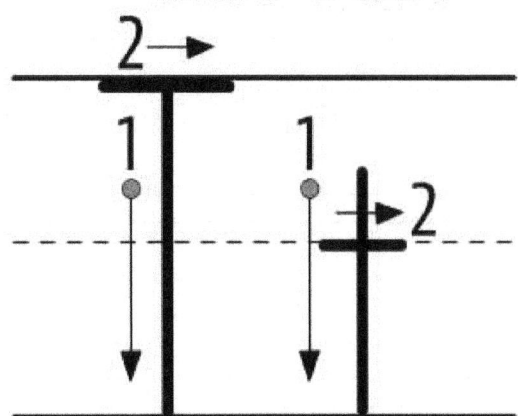

I Know My Letter:

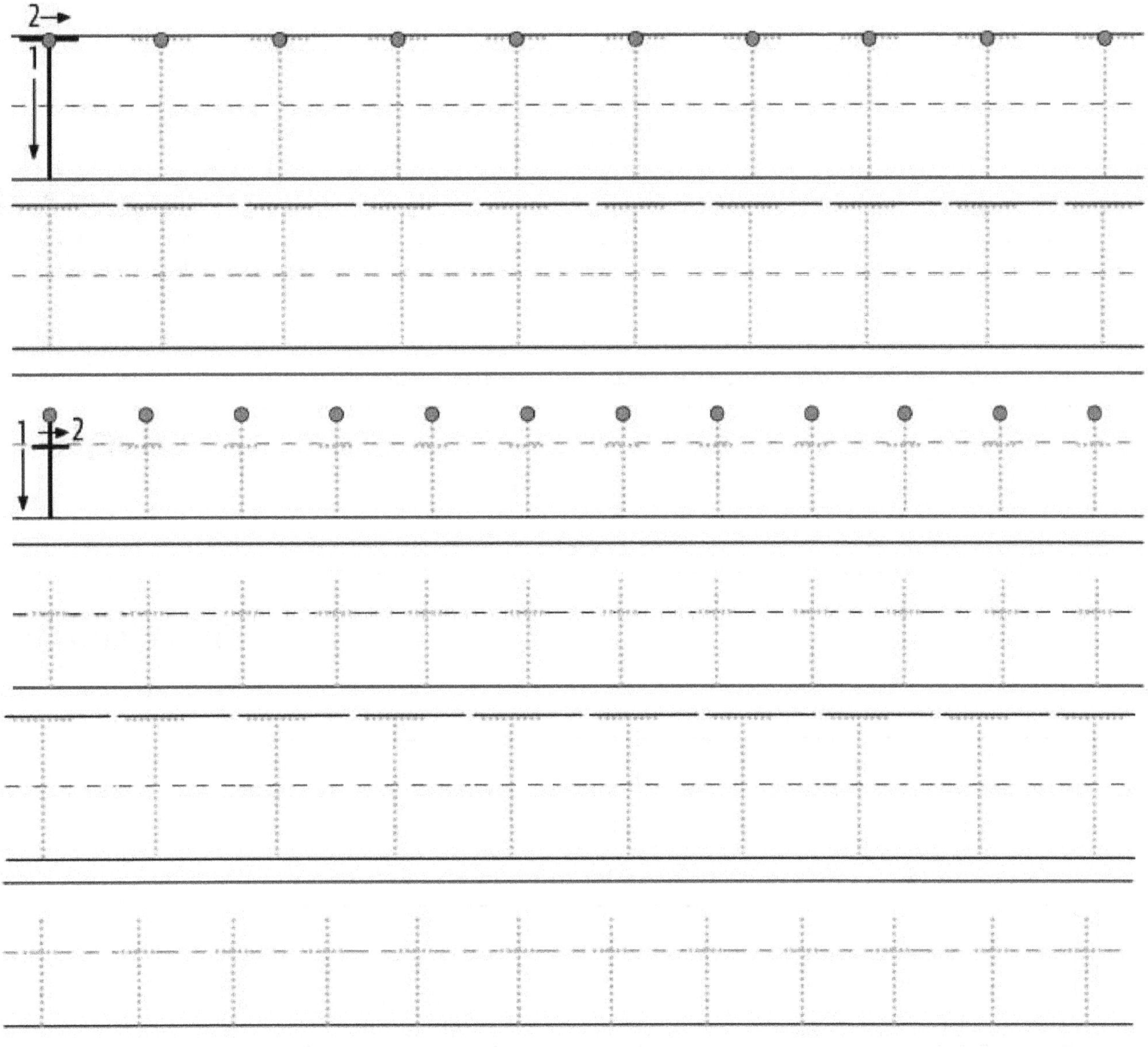

PRACTICE!   PRACTICE!   PRACTICE!

Tiger

Turtle

Trace and Color

PRACTICE! PRACTICE! PRACTICE!

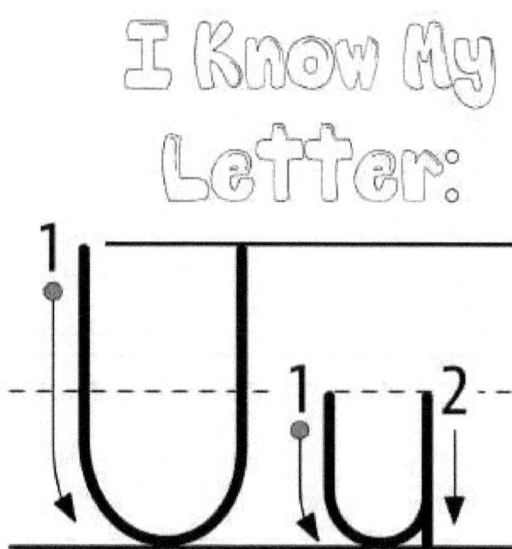

I Know My Letter:

U is for Unicorn

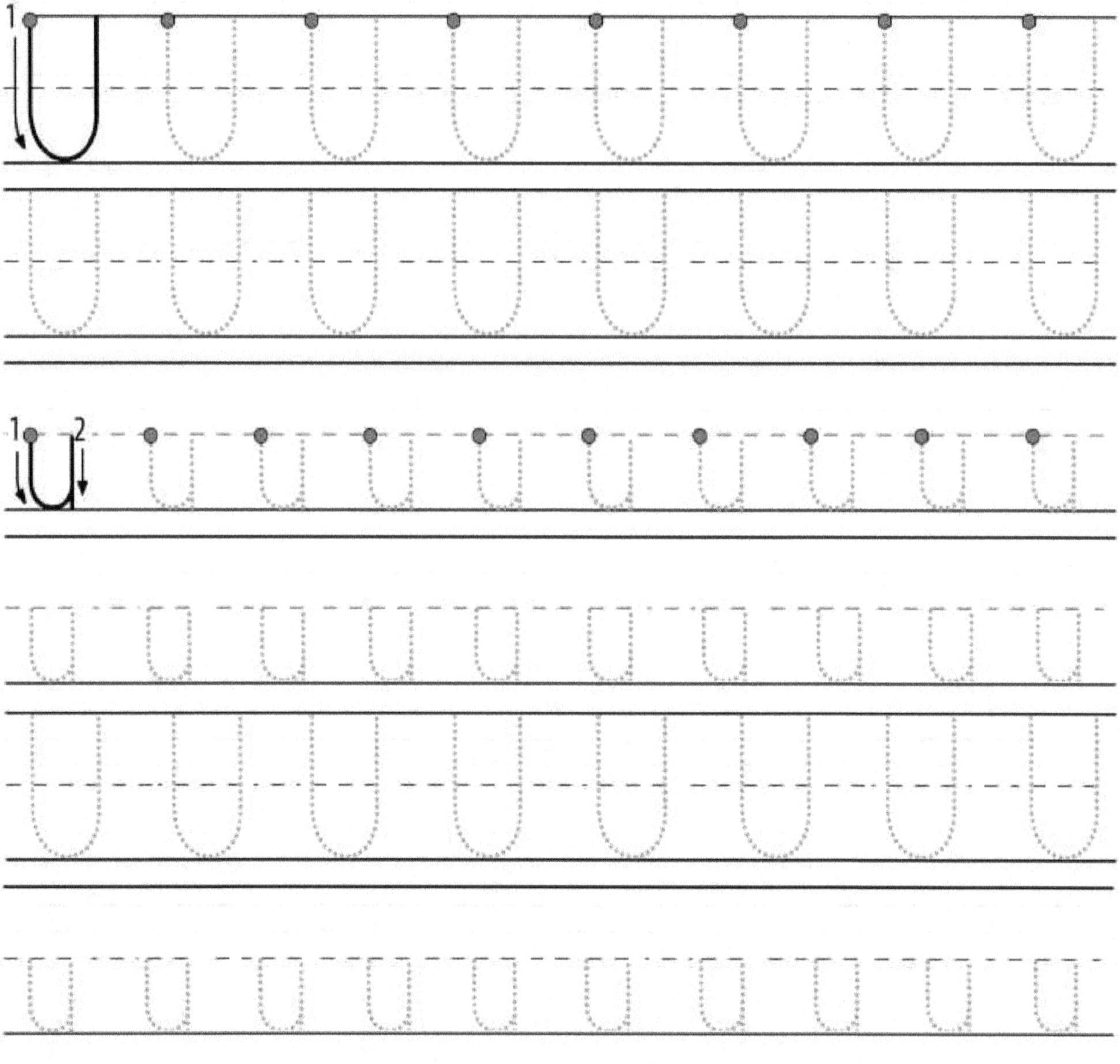

PRACTICE! PRACTICE! PRACTICE!

Unicycle

Umbrella

Trace and Color

PRACTICE! PRACTICE! PRACTICE!

V is for Violin

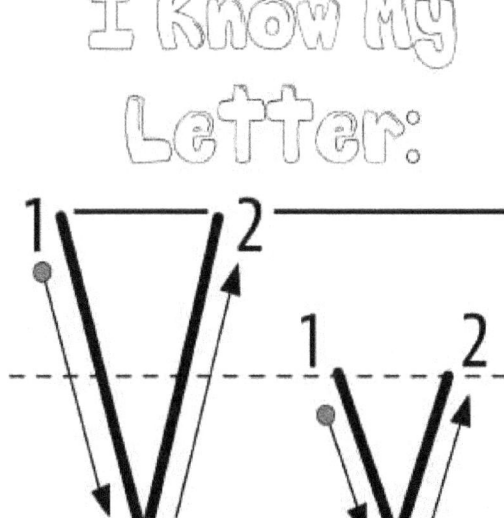

I Know My Letter:

PRACTICE! PRACTICE! PRACTICE!

Vase

Vulture

Trace and Color

PRACTICE! PRACTICE! PRACTICE!

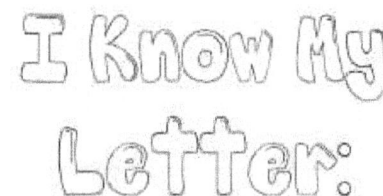

I Know My Letter:

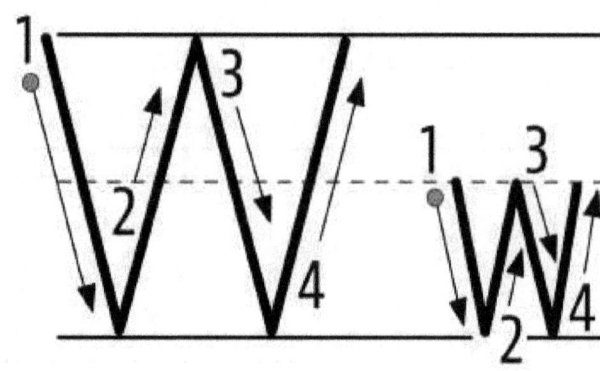

W is for Window

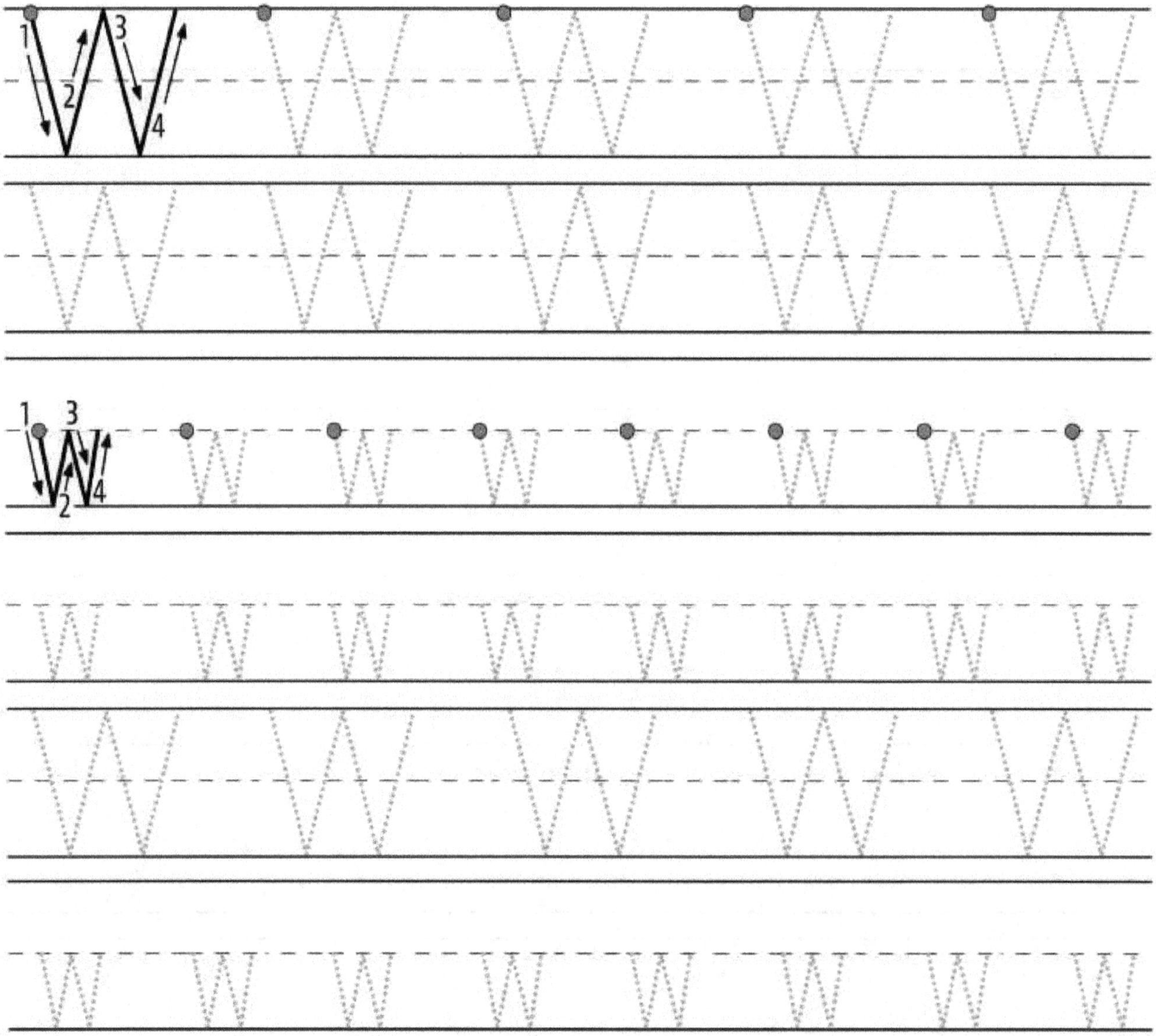

PRACTICE! PRACTICE! PRACTICE!

Watermelon

Whale

Trace and Color

PRACTICE!　　　　　　PRACTICE!　　　　　　PRACTICE!

I Know My Letter:

X is for Xylophone

X X X X X X X X

X X X X X X X X

x x x x x x x x x x

x x x x x x x x x x

X X X X X X X X

x x x x x x x x x x

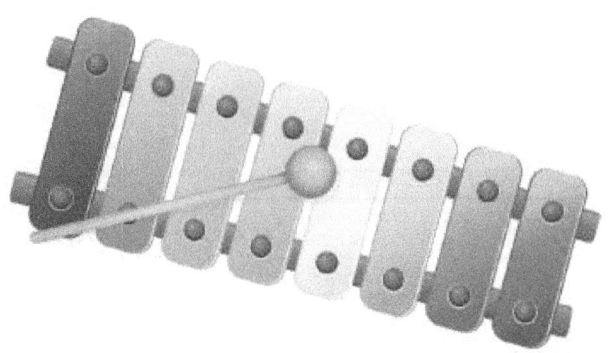

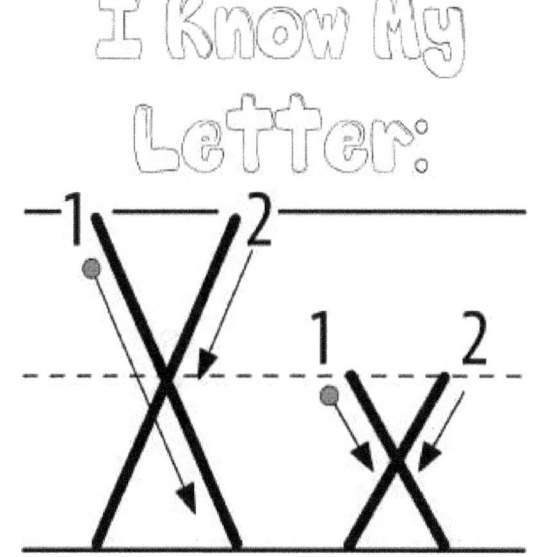

PRACTICE! PRACTICE! PRACTICE!

X-mas Tree

X-ray Fish

Trace and Color

PRACTICE!   PRACTICE!   PRACTICE!

Y is for Yarn

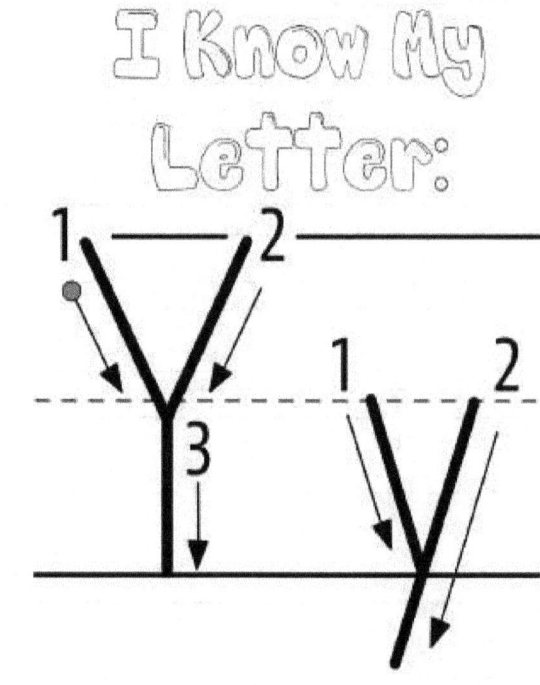

I Know My Letter:

PRACTICE!   PRACTICE!   PRACTICE!

Yak

Yolk

Trace and Color

PRACTICE!   PRACTICE!   PRACTICE!

Z is for Zebra

I Know My Letter:

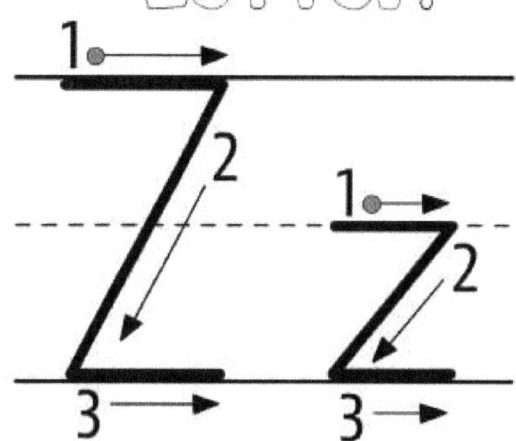

PRACTICE! PRACTICE! PRACTICE!

Zeppelin

Zipper

Trace and Color

PRACTICE! PRACTICE! PRACTICE!

PART II

SIGHT WORD

Learn to read and write

SIGHT WORD PRACTICE

Color in the word	Trace the word
my	my

Find and circle the sight word

I love my dad   store   my   the   for

tee   at   to   I want to dye my hair black   can

Checkout my new watch   my then   I love my mom

Write the word

Write the word in a sentence

I want to write _____ name.

SIGHT WORD PRACTICE

Color in the word	Trace the word
and	and

Find and circle the sight word

He runs so fast and so does she   ant   bite   and

me   and   by   the   Snake and Lion are wild animals

      not   You and I are best friends   and   time

Write the word

Write the word in a sentence

You _____ I are little kids.

SIGHT WORD PRACTICE

Color in the word	Trace the word
the	the

Find and circle the sight word

I can see the cat and dog   ant   the and

me   the   by   at   Where is the toy?   then look

   not   You are the best kid in class   the time

Write the word

Write the word in a sentence

Look, _____ sun is red.

SIGHT WORD PRACTICE

Color in the word	Trace the word
can	can

Find and circle the sight word

I can read and write english   could   can   cake   would

cat   can   by   the   Tell me what you can do

   not   If I can I would help you out   can   time

Write the word

| | | |

Write the word in a sentence

Yes, we _____ play together.

SIGHT WORD PRACTICE

Color in the word	Trace the word
for	for

Find and circle the sight word

Who are you waiting for ?   from far for

them   for   at   fat   When would you come for me?

fish   I use cup for drinking water   for   time

Write the word

Write the word in a sentence

I have a gift _____ you.

SIGHT WORD PRACTICE

Color in the word	Trace the word
big	big

Find and circle the sight word

My God is a big God   mouse   cut   big

you   big   at   the   I leave in a big house   wild   hen

either   I saw a big fish in the water   big   time

Write the word

Write the word in a sentence

My school is very _____

SIGHT WORD PRACTICE

Color in the word	Trace the word
at	at

Find and circle the sight word

I was at my friend's house today   bee   antelope   at

for   at   by   but   We live at harry street california

when   I would be waiting at the bus station   at   clock

Write the word

Write the word in a sentence

I am _____ home.

SIGHT WORD PRACTICE

Color in the word	Trace the word
up	up

Find and circle the sight word

The house went up in flames   cut   bud   up

cup   up   at   the   Get up from your bed

pop   Look up into the clouds   up   shot

Write the word

Write the word in a sentence

Dad was caught _____ in traffic

SIGHT WORD PRACTICE

Color in the word	Trace the word
said	said

Find and circle the sight word

She said it was alright   over   run   said   go   but

take   said   with   the   He said that we can dance

at   I said I am very tired   said   blue   then

Write the word

Write the word in a sentence

I _____ I would try my best.

SIGHT WORD PRACTICE

Color in the word	Trace the word
does	does

Find and circle the sight word

She does her chores   cat   many does   use

can   does   dad   the   He does his homework after school

not   My mom always does her best for me   does

Write the word

Write the word in a sentence

It _____ not matter to me.

SIGHT WORD PRACTICE

Color in the word	Trace the word
one	one

Find and circle the sight word

Do you have one more?   down   go   one

but   one   once   the   Mom and dad are my one and only

when   I would give you one of my toys   that   one

Write the word

Write the word in a sentence

I am _____ year older.

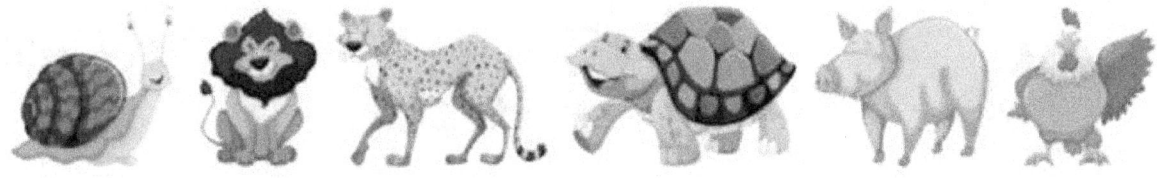

SIGHT WORD PRACTICE

Color in the word	Trace the word
write	write

Find and circle the sight word

Let us write a story together   water   down   write   white

maybe   write   right   yes   Can you write your name?

red   My mom taught me how to write   time   write

Write the word

Write the word in a sentence

I can _____ english very well.

SIGHT WORD PRACTICE

Color in the word	Trace the word
was	was

Find and circle the sight word

He ate so fast because he was very hungry   does   was

war   bite   was   and   I was at my aunty's house   dog

me   was   while   the   Yesterday was Monday

Write the word

Write the word in a sentence

I _____ angry at her.

SIGHT WORD PRACTICE

Color in the word	Trace the word
read	read

Find and circle the sight word

I am learning to read and write   does   was   read

learn   read   bite   Mom, please read animal farm for me

me   right   the   Can you read my handwritting?   hat   read

Write the word

Write the word in a sentence

Can you _____ what is written?

SIGHT WORD PRACTICE

Color in the word	Trace the word
been	been

Find and circle the sight word

What have you been reading?   does   been   being

being   We have been living here for long   dog   been

me   been   be   I have been happy with my new school

Write the word

_____

Write the word in a sentence

He has _____ my best friend

SIGHT WORD PRACTICE

Color in the word	Trace the word
what	what

Find and circle the sight word

She told me what I need to do   wine   was   what   why

with   war   I told him what he wants to hear   dog   what

what   was   winter   the   Yesterday was what?

Write the word

Write the word in a sentence

You know _____ I want for a gift.

SIGHT WORD PRACTICE

Color in the word	Trace the word
when	when

Find and circle the sight word

I don't know when   then   hen   what   water   when

den   ben   when   and   Did they say when?   donkey

when   them   while   the   Go when you want

Write the word

Write the word in a sentence

Mom, _____ is breakfast?

SIGHT WORD PRACTICE

Color in the word	Trace the word
after	after

Find and circle the sight word

He went after her   does   after   afterthought

afternoon   after   sun   Come to my house after school

We went home after church serivce was concluded   dog

Write the word

Write the word in a sentence

I was sad _____ mom left home.

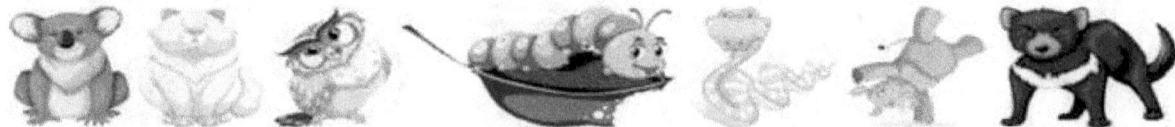

SIGHT WORD PRACTICE

Color in the word	Trace the word
go	go

Find and circle the sight word

Let's go home   went   go   gone   arrive

war   come   go   and   I want to go to steve's house   dog

now   go   while   the   We should go see a movie

Write the word

Write the word in a sentence

Let's _____ to disney land

SIGHT WORD PRACTICE

Color in the word	Trace the word
had	had

Find and circle the sight word

Ben and I have had breakfast   having   has   was   had

went had bite   He had told me he won't come to school

dog   had My mom had to take me to school

Write the word

H

Write the word in a sentence

I _____ to tell dad the truth.

SIGHT WORD PRACTICE

Color in the word	Trace the word
any	any

Find and circle the sight word

Is there any milk left at the supermarket?   and   yes   any

   with   ant   any   and   I wasn't with any of them   dog

any was car   while   any   the   Come with any of those

Write the word

Write the word in a sentence

I don't want _____ of the toys.

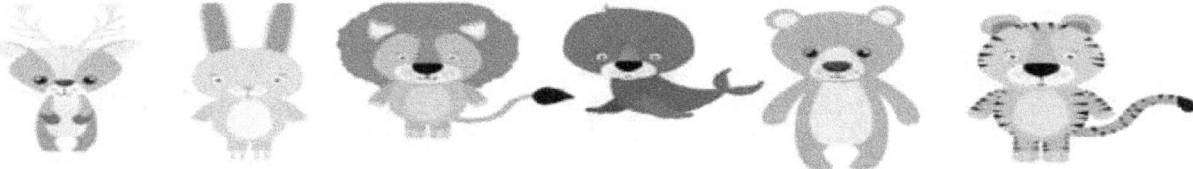

SIGHT WORD PRACTICE

Color in the word	Trace the word
new	new

Find and circle the sight word

I have a new toy   pet   teeth   was   new

turtle   bite   new   at   I love my new dog pet   new

me   was   while   the   Dad bought a new car for mom

Write the word

Write the word in a sentence

I want a _____ toy

SIGHT WORD PRACTICE

Color in the word	Trace the word
song	song

Find and circle the sight word

Can you please sing a song for me?   sung singing   song

music   yes   at   song   instrument

song   school   was   My best song is row row row your boat

Write the word

Write the word in a sentence

Dad sang a _____ for me.

SIGHT WORD PRACTICE

Color in the word	Trace the word
hear	hear

Find and circle the sight word

I can hear you loud and clear   was   does   ear   here   hear

bite   now   hear   head   John can't hear with his ears

my aunty's house   dog   Did you hear what he said?

Write the word

Write the word in a sentence

I can _____ with both my ears.

SIGHT WORD PRACTICE

Color in the word	Trace the word
but	but

Find and circle the sight word

Don't tell anyone but your sister   button   was   and   but

burn   bite   but   why   It's sad, but true   dog

when   but   after   Tom tried, but failed

Write the word

but

Write the word in a sentence

Thanks, _____ no thanks.

SIGHT WORD PRACTICE

Color in the word	Trace the word
is	is

Find and circle the sight word

Where is my dog?   cat   dig   are   his   is

at   is   and   What I want is my mom and dad   house   is

me   was   school   the   Today is Sunday

Write the word

Write the word in a sentence

My math teacher _____ the best.

CONGRATULATIONS!

Congratulations for transiting the pages of this workbook from start to finish, and it is my deepest desire that you found it helpful and at the same time fun.

Many readers do not know how hard reviews are to come by and how much they help an author. So, if you liked this book, I would be incredibly grateful if you could take just 60 seconds to write a short review on Amazon, even if it is a few sentences.

Thanks for the time taken to share your thoughts!